INSPECTOR SMART AND THE CASE OF THE EMPTY TOMB

Written by Michael J Tinker

Illustrated by Isaac Stovell

Published by

thegoodbook
COMPANY

Note:

Inspector Smart is an **imaginary** character, but the people he interviews are **real** (though we don't know the names of the Roman soldiers, so we invented those). They lived 2000 years ago in the days of ancient Rome, at the time of the **very first Easter**. You can read about them in the **Bible** (see page 24).

Inspector Smart and The Case of the Empty Tomb
© Michael J Tinker/The Good Book Company, 2014

Illustrations by Isaac Stovell

Published by
The Good Book Company Ltd

Tel (UK): 0333 123 0880
International: +44 (0) 208 942 0880
Email: info@thegoodbook.co.uk

Websites:
UK: www.thegoodbook.co.uk
North America: www.thegoodbook.com
Australia: www.thegoodbook.com.au
New Zealand: www.thegoodbook.co.nz

ISBN: 9781909919648

the good book COMPANY

Design and cover illustration by André Parker
Printed in the Czech Republic

Inspector Smart sat at his desk looking over a very interesting case he had just been handed.

It said:

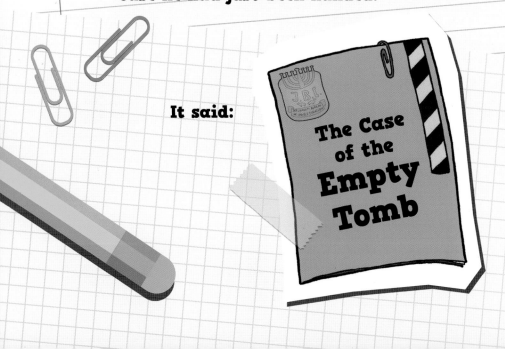

The Case of the **Empty Tomb**

According to the file there was a man called **Jesus**, who had done some strange things.

Normally when people are **sick**, they call a doctor and the doctor gives them some medicine to try and make them better again. But Jesus could make people better simply by **speaking!**

Fig 01

Fig 02

Normally when people want to cross some water, they walk on a bridge. But Jesus could cross a lake by walking **on the water** itself!

And normally when people die, they stay dead. But Jesus had raised a little girl to life simply by telling her to **get up!**

Fig 03

"Interesting"
thought Inspector Smart.

Then something sad happened. Jesus was treated like a criminal, sent to court and **killed.**

Fig 04

Jesus had said he was the **King**, but the people didn't want him to be King.

But this is where the case got really **interesting...**

Jesus had been put in a cave – the place where they put people who had died. A **huge stone** had been rolled across the door of the cave and **armed men** stood guard to make sure no one stole Jesus' body.

Fig 05

But when some women got to the tomb on Sunday, the guards were **gone**, the stone had been **rolled away** and the tomb was...

empty!

"Very interesting," thought Inspector Smart. It was time to do some investigating.

Inspector Smart got into his super-duper police chariot pulled by his trusty horse, **Bob**...

and rode off into **Jerusalem.**

Inspector Smart came to a **huge house**. In fact it was more like a **castle** than a house. Outside were two guards, who saluted as Inspector Smart got down from his super-duper police chariot.

"I'm here to see the General,"
said Smart.

"Yes Sir! Right away Sir!"
replied one of the guards.

Within moments Smart had been marched into the house and was sitting down having a cup of tea with the General.

Smart spoke first. "General, I wonder if you could tell me about **the day Jesus died.** Some people are saying that he's alive again. And we all know that dead people **don't** come alive again. I was thinking — perhaps Jesus didn't really die."

"Inspector Smart – that's **not very smart** of you," said the General.

"We Romans are **excellent** at killing people. I know it doesn't sound very nice but that's what we do. I'm sad to say that Jesus was **definitely dead**. I rather liked the man. He seemed so kind and even said he **forgave us** for killing him."

"I've never seen anyone like him. But a job's a job. We were told to execute him, so that's what we did."

Inspector Smart finished his cup of tea and, after being shown the General's rather large **collection of medals**, he said goodbye and left.

This case wasn't over yet!

Next, Inspector Smart decided he needed to chat to one of the women who went to the tomb. **Mary Magdalene** lived in the centre of town. Although Smart's super-duper police chariot was super-duper fast, even Bob couldn't whizz past **all the traffic** clogging Jerusalem's streets.

Finally, Smart arrived at **Mary's house.**

It was a humble and pleasant apartment. Smart sat down on a **comfy chair** and sipped at another cup of tea.

Mary began...

"It was early on the **Sunday morning**. My friends and I went to the tomb of Jesus to put **special perfume** on the body to stop it smelling bad. It's what you have to do in a hot country."

"We were wondering who was going to help us move that huge stone they had put in front of the tomb. But when we got there, we found that it had **already been moved**. We edged closer to the tomb to find out what was going on and, to our horror, we found that the tomb was... empty!"

"**Jesus' body had gone!**"

"At that stage we didn't think that **Jesus was alive**. Dead people don't come alive, right? We thought somebody had **taken the body** away."

"I went off to one part of the garden and I was **in tears**. Why would anyone take Jesus' body away? It was cruel. Then a man came up to me and said: '**Why are you crying?**' I thought it was the gardener. If anyone knew where Jesus was it would be him, so I said:

"If you know where they've taken Jesus, **please tell me!**"

"Then he said: 'Mary'."

"And then I knew – it was Jesus!"

"It really was. Jesus was standing right in front of me. I wanted to **hug him** and **never let him go**. But he said I had to go and **tell everyone** else that he's alive. So that's what I did."

"Hmmm..." thought Inspector Smart.

This was getting **stranger and stranger**. First of all, Jesus had definitely died. The General had said it, and even Mary thought Jesus was dead. None of them expected him to be walking around.

But then something had happened, and Mary was saying **she had met Jesus!**

"Thank you for the tea, Mary. I've got to go and see **one more person**," said Inspector Smart.

"Who's that?" asked Mary.

"Your friend **Thomas** — the one who won't believe anything unless he sees it for himself..."

On the way to **Thomas' house** Inspector Smart started to think. So far it looked as if **Jesus had come alive**.

All the **evidence** was pointing to it. But what did it all mean? **Why** did Jesus die and then come alive again?

This case wasn't over yet!

Thomas was a **small** man but with a **stern** look in his eyes.

HE-BREW
best tea
in Israel

This was **not** a man who would be **easily fooled**.

Slurping down a rather strong cup of **Yorkshire tea**, Thomas began his story.

"When people were saying **Jerusalem United** would **win the cup**, I said: 'I'll believe **that** when I **see** it'."

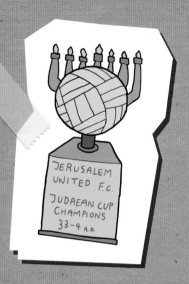

"When people said that one day we'll **fly in the sky**, I said: 'I'll believe **that** when I **see** it'."

"When people said **Jesus is alive**, I said:

"I'll believe that when I see it."

"One day I was **with the others**. They had been going on about Jesus being **alive**, but I'm not going to believe that kind of thing unless I see it with my **own eyes**. Dead people don't come alive again, **right?**"

"That particular day I was **proved wrong**. As we were talking, **Jesus** suddenly appeared in the room. **Right in front of me!**"

"He said: 'Touch my hands — **see**, they're the same ones that had nails put through them. **Stop doubting** and **believe**'."

"I didn't need any more proof. I said to Jesus: 'My Lord and my God'."

"What else could I say?"

"Jesus had **said to us** before that he was going to be killed and then **come alive again**. But we didn't believe him."

"He said he had to die **for us** so we could be **friends with God** again."

"And that's what he did. He did it so we could be **forgiven** for trying to be in charge of our own lives."

"Now, I don't know about you, but I can't think of **anyone better** to be in charge of my life."

"**Jesus is my Lord and my God.**"

"This is **beyond** interesting," thought Inspector Smart. "This is **life-changing**."

Back at his office, Inspector Smart finished writing up his report.

Jesus had **definitely** died. Normally dead people don't come alive again.

But Jesus had. All the evidence pointed to it.

No one has power over death except **God himself**.

Inspector Smart realised that this wasn't **just** an interesting mystery.

He couldn't write **"Jesus is alive"** and then **close** the case.

Jesus had died **for us**. He had made it possible for us to be **friends** with God!

And he had come alive again and is the **King**.

This case now involved **Inspector Smart himself**, because when you find out that Jesus is alive you have to decide — will you say: **"My Lord and my God"** like Thomas did?

There was **only one** conclusion Inspector Smart could make.

He had some **praying** to do.

Dear God,

I know that I have tried to be **in charge** of my own life and that I need to be **forgiven**.

Thank you for sending Jesus to die for me.

Thank you that Jesus came **alive again** to be the King.

I want Jesus to be **my Lord and my God**.

Thank you for helping me to become **your friend**.

Amen

All of the **evidence** Inspector Smart investigated comes from **the Bible**. Read about the **very first Easter** and meet some of the people who were there at the time, including Mary Magdalene, the Roman guards and Thomas.

You can read the Bible story for yourself on our special **"Smart Sheet"**, free to download from the websites below.

INSPECTOR SMART'S AND THE CASE OF

THE EMPTY TOMB!

All of the evidence Inspector Smart investigated comes from the Bible. You can read all about the life of Jesus in four books (called Gospels) that were written by Matthew, Mark, Luke and John. Between them they tell us the whole of the Easter story. Here are some of the Bible passages that show us the evidence that Jesus died and came alive again. They start on the Thursday evening of the very first Easter week.

INSPECTOR SMART'S AND THE CASE OF THE EMPTY TOMB!

CASE FILE

BY TIM CHESTER

You'll also find details of the "Inspector Smart and the Empty Tomb Case File" and other items in the Inspector Smart range.

www.thegoodbook.co.uk/smart

www.thegoodbook.com/smart
www.thegoodbook.com.au/smart
www.thegoodbook.co.nz/smart